OVERCOME

SOCIAL ANXIETY

CURE SHYNESS AND
TALK TO ANYONE WITH CONFIDENCE

BY ADAM ROCKMAN

WWW.EVOLVETOWIN.COM

Contents

Thank you for purchasing this book!

As a surprise bonus I'm giving you another book completely free!

How to Overcome Fear focuses on the 8 Essential Steps to overcoming any fear.

Go to www.EvolveToWin.com to get your free copy now!

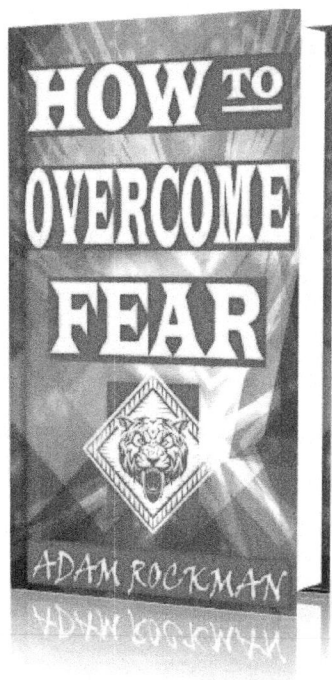

Introduction

Except for psychopaths, and those extremely practiced at overcoming fear, everyone experiences some level of social anxiety.

A healthy level of social anxiety helps people maintain acceptance in and benefit from living among others. If you break too many norms, or anger the wrong people you could be kicked out of your community. When we first started living in groups that abandonment could mean death.

When you are a child you feel the same threat to losing social approval. If you misbehave your parents may insist you change your behavior. If they insist with enough anger, it might scare you out of feeling comfortable expressing yourself to them. This is the beginning of social anxiety.

You don't want to disappoint your parents because if you did it could threaten your existence. You were worried they would stop caring about you and abandon you. So you conform when they yell at you for speaking too loudly in public, or causing any other problems.

In healthy doses this encourages you to behave in socially acceptable ways and prepares you for socializing with your future classmates and friends.

When you get to school however, there is even more pressure from teachers and classmates to conform to the norms of your groups. You start paying for accepting by selling bits of your individuality.

This is a normal process. A lot of people come out of it capable of both expressing themselves and being considerate to expectations of the people around them.

They still feel a bit of social anxiety in certain situations, but usually they feel comfortable expressing their own opinion without fear of being judged or rejected.

For many people however, social pressure feels like a massive boulder squashing every bit of individuality into a weak paste of social failure.

If you are reading this book, you likely feel this excessive level of social anxiety. You want to express yourself but worry it would mean risking rejection and judgement from others.

If you really want social confidence you will need to face your fears. You will need to break bad habits and think about why you developed them in the first place.

That vulnerability will become a strength.

Some people suggest you "fake it until you make it." This barely helps, because you might not believe the confident actions you are intimidating.

You can fix the symptoms of social anxiety but if you haven't handled your deeper feelings of inadequacy people easily see through the fake façade. At least socially intelligent people usually do.

I suspect that "fake it until you make it supporters" have never had to deal with crippling social anxiety before. They've never been so terrified of strangers that they avoid eye contact, answering the phone and even leaving home.

They are giving that lame line of advice to people who already have a bit of confidence and just want a bit more. But we know social anxiety can be much more complex and needs more than pretend courage to resolve.

The theory is that eventually these habits will become your natural way of expressing yourself. That may be helpful but it is not enough. There are internal issues to resolve and pain to let go of before you can feel genuinely confident with others.

Fearing rejection and judgement is a major reason for social anxiety. In fact, it is the definition of social anxiety. The only other thing you could be afraid of is being physically attacked. Which is still a form of rejection and is extremely unlikely in most cases.

As mentioned earlier, everyone experiences some level of social anxiety. All normal people desire acceptance and to avoid rejection. If your mind is healthy this means since you would like to be accepted and avoid rejection you will speak politely instead of sharing every insulting thought that comes into your imagination.

This filter of restraint helps you to hold back things you know would likely produce rejection.

For example you see a female colleague you need to get along with to successfully complete your work. Instead of calling her a fat cow you choose to talk to her about the weather or some other boring topic people in offices discuss to avoid actually opening up with each other.

This filter is a natural part of the human brain and you should be happy you have it. Without it we wouldn't be able to lie to protect each other from the truth of our real opinions. It's the glue that keeps society and world's entire economy running.

In the healthy, well-adjusted mind, your filter prevents social disasters that could prevent you from getting a job, finding a mate and pursuing any goal that interests you.

The filter influences your behavior based on what you let through it.

If you socialize often, you learn to relax in these situations. Because you have accepted that talking to people usually isn't so difficult. And the more you practice, the easier it becomes.

But of course the opposite is also true. Every time you avoid a social situation, you are associating pain and fear with interacting with others. Every time you avoid eye contact, hold back an opinion, don't assert yourself, and so on, you are reinforcing social anxiety.

How terrifying is that?

How many hundreds or thousands of interactions have you avoided?

Each avoidance is like a noose slowly shrinking your comfort zone until you find it's around your neck.

So what's the cure?

The obvious answer is to invest in the opposite behavior of course!

This reinforces the belief that it is safe to interact with others.

This can be effective on its own. But we will discuss even more effective advice throughout this book.

A Confident Mindset

You may not know why you feel severe social anxiety.

It usually starts in childhood. Some classmate may have made fun of you, so you start to get scared of sharing your opinion. Eventually that early memory has completely faded. But the habit of avoidance is still with you. Because you've constantly reinforced it.

The desire to be accepted is a very powerful motivation. Socially anxiety people are often paralyzed in social situations because they face a paradox.

They want to be accepted and loved by everyone.

But that is impossible.

They may not be capable of articulating that fact, but it is often true. They inevitably choose to say nothing instead of saying something that could potentially lead to rejection. Or when they try to open their mouth to speak their worry makes them stutter in low volume and they often need to repeat themselves.

It's really ironic actually. To avoid rejection through silence makes you less likable and therefore more likely to be rejected.

Recognizing this paradox is the first step to resolving social anxiety.

The next, is to acknowledge that rejection is completely acceptable. You are free to reject other people, so why shouldn't other people be free to reject you?

Imagine you try to talk to someone at a party but they aren't interested.

Is something wrong with you?

Don't all people want to be close to you?

Are you going to give up socializing for the day and go home feeling bad?

You likely could have talked to more people and had really enjoyable interactions.

But since you failed to prove to yourself that every single person loves you it somehow means there is no way to cope with this failure!

You feel like giving up on humanity and abstaining from bathing for a few weeks while you are scared to answer the door no matter who shows up.

That exaggerated consequence is exactly the baseless paranoia that leads many people to avoid social situations that would actually lead to developing confidence.

It's the fear of confronting the truth of their imperfection.

The fear that not everyone finds them attractive.

The fear of not being good enough.

For some people this fear is so severe they are terrified of leaving their home and interacting with anyone.

You might not articulate these fears in exactly these words, but the significance is still there.

Many social anxiety sufferers complain that others just don't like them. They complain that nobody pays attention or listens to them. They feel the world is completely unfair and some people just get extra attention and acceptance without any reason at all.

These same social anxiety sufferers whine about how other people are inconsiderate, selfish scum who never think about including others.

They are so desperate for approval from everyone that they can't recognize these complaints as manifestations of their own feelings of inadequacy.

They feel like they aren't good enough to gain the acceptance of others, so they are desperate for signs of acceptance and rejection. When they are included in something they care about they feel validated. But when someone politely offers constructive criticism it can ruin their entire life.

This is because their life is often built on the validation others provide them. They would only feel happy if everyone respected their every thought. But they know that's impossible so they are scared to stick a toe in the cold water of the social swimming pool.

The truth is you don't need to be loved by every person.

You don't need everyone to praise your every word.

When you honestly express your ideas there will be people who don't like it. But so what? There will still be other people who respect you courage to be authentic. Those are the people you should make friends with.

If you try to make friends with everyone, you can only make friends with no one.

One bad interaction is not the end of your world. Even if your feelings hurt, it's like going to the gym. Your emotional resilience will get stronger.

Though in the same way working out way too much can be more harmful than helpful, too much intense negativity from others can also hold back your ability to believe in yourself.

But that is no excuse to mistakenly assume one or two rejections is too much.

When rejection happens, reflect on your pain later when there are no opportunities for acceptance or rejection.

This means for example, if you are at a party and have a bad interaction, don't give up. Keep meeting people and when the event is over take a moment to think about your reactions to each interaction and what it means to you.

When you give up on enjoyable social interactions because you didn't get your desired outcome you reinforce negative beliefs about yourself.

If however, you instead choose to ignore rejection and keep enjoying the opportunity to express yourself with other people, you gradually reinforce the belief that you don't need everyone's acceptance to feel happy.

This frees you to socialize with anyone you want to meet because you aren't desperate for their approval.

This should make completely logical sense to you. However, if your social anxiety is severe enough you may still be skeptical because you still feel that heavy weight in your chest or throat that is a symptom of negative beliefs in your own unworthiness.

In general, people rely more on their emotions than rational thought when making decisions. If you feel like the world hates you then no matter how much contrary evidence I show you it won't change your beliefs.

I could show you videos of people smiling when you talk to them, listening intently to your every word, and even praising you. But for habitually negative people they still often wouldn't be convinced of their likability. If they really want to believe nobody could ever like them, there is no way of convincing them otherwise even when the evidence clearly shows the opposite conclusion.

People believe whatever they want to believe. The beliefs protect them from admitting their own flaws and inadequacies. They want to believe that they are paragons of perfection but it is other people who can't recognize how awesome they are.

You'll have to practice opening your mind to the truth if you really want to change these negative beliefs.

Imagine your life had been filled with 100% praise, respect and overenthusiastic approval of everything you do.

What kind of person do you think you would become. Many people assume this leads to confidence. In fact a person with this kind of life may appear on the surface to be very courageous. After all he can say whatever he wants without fear of rejection. He knows everything he says will be accepted.

But this is a very weak form of confidence. What if one day people ridicule his ideas?

His entire personality would shatter!

Because it is based on all the approval people give him.

When you base your identity only on what other people think of you it is not confidence. It is weak dependence on a meaningless source of validation.

Real confidence comes not only from social approval, but also from the knowledge that you can overcome the inevitable challenges and rejections of social interactions.

Validation based confidence is easily broken. As long as people accept you, you feel great. But once someone doesn't acknowledge you, it can feel like the end of the world.

The problem is you don't have enough references of risking social rejection and accepting the consequences. You've already assumed rejection without even trying. That becomes your usual state of mind.

Whenever you get approval, the brain releases a burst of serotonin and similar neurotransmitters that improve your mood. If you ever have a fun day of socializing in the evening you might have trouble sleeping because you feel like you have more energy than usual. Positive social interaction is very healthy for the mind and body.

Studies have even shown that people who socialize more live longer. When you live a life terrified of interacting with anyone you miss out on all those benefits.

People who've never faced adversity in their life get those benefits by the continual approval of others. But at soon as you throw the tiniest or problems or criticisms at them, they get depressed, angry or emotional.

This is common in many affluent families where children grow up without experiencing real challenges or threats to their confidence. Rates of drug abuse are much higher among affluent youth than their poorer peers in the same communities. Psychologists conclude that this is largely a coping mechanism to handle their inability to handle the inevitable adversity and pain of life.

The truth is rejection in all its forms helps you grow.

It really does build character.

Facing fears helped me build confidence and made me a much better man. I now welcome these experiences because I know they help me level up.

You can't just live an isolated life hidden away from the dangers of running into obnoxious people who will reject you. It will only retard your growth and leave you stuck in an immature level of development. Don't run away from the lessons life is trying to teach you.

The only result is an unlived life.

Imagine you get to the end of your life. You are too weak to stand up. You can only lie there reflecting on your life. Think about the people you've met. Think about all your regrets. All the times you could have faced a fear but you didn't take action.

Think about the people you never got to share your real feelings with. Think about the relationships you missed out on. Think about the relationships you stayed in out of fear. Think about all the opportunities you missed.

Think about how every chance you got to change yourself you instead chose to take the lazy route and just stagnate instead of taking action.

It's all over. You could have become a very confident person. But you gave up all the opportunities to develop confidence.

It's time to say goodbye to this life that you never actually lived.

As you are leaving, you get a glimpse at how your life could have looked like if you had taken more action.

You see yourself facing fears. It's painful, but eventually that version of yourself is happy and free, has lots of friends, and success in every area of life. How painful does it feel to know your life could have been completely different?

But what if you could come back and start over? Would you?

From this moment on you can see social anxiety as an opportunity for growth. As you gain experience your life will change!

You get another chance at life! Will you waste it this time too?

Your entire life is a result of the decisions you make. Make the decision to interact with the world no matter how awkward it may feel at times. When life presents the choice between growth and stagnation you know which to choose.

Social anxiety is a physical sensation that tempts you to hide from social interaction. The fear of rejection or fear of being judged is actually an opportunity to train yourself. When you have a chance to talk to someone but you are too scared to even say "hi" this avoidance only trains a habit of avoiding social interaction. However when you force yourself to talk to a new person it reinforces the belief that social interaction is easy.

You can start to believe in your ability to handle a variety of social situations.

Give up attachment to your anxious identity

You have inevitably encountered people who make absolute statements such as "I suffer from social anxiety." "Nobody likes talking to me." or, "I ALWAYS feel nervous around people. I CAN'T cure it."

They've already accepted anxiety as who they are and aren't willing to change. It's a self-fulfilling prophecy.

If you believe you are social anxious and can't talk to people that's exactly how you will behave.

If you define yourself as an anxious person then you are scared to give up this identity by facing fears and becoming confident. I refuse to make statements like "I suffer from social anxiety… (Or some other psychological condition). Social anxiety can be effectively treated. But if you close your mind to treatment, you can never fix yourself.

Your thoughts and emotions do not define you. You experience anxious thoughts, but that doesn't make you an "anxious, fearful person." There must be some times where you feel confidence and relaxed interacting with others. But you may ignore those experiences because they don't confirm this desire to be the "anxious person."

Detach yourself from these anxious thoughts and feelings. Recognize that you are the awareness experiencing them and that there is a huge range of more positive emotions that you could alternatively experience.

By doing this, you can start getting to know your true self and have more conscious control over redefining who you want to be.

10 Best Ways to

Overcome Social Anxiety

So we've established why facing your fears is one of if not THE most important ingredients to overcoming social anxiety.

It will be uncomfortable at first, so this chapter provides 10 helpful tools for the challenge of building new, confident social habits.

I go into much more detail about each of these tools in my book **Social Confidence Mastery: How to Eliminate Social Anxiety, Insecurities, Shyness, And The Fear of Rejection.**

Check it out if you want even more great advice on improving your confidence in social situations. It even includes a 10 day plan for overcoming your fears and building confidence. I've used it with dozens of clients I've coached and it always gets great results.

Here are 10 Tips that should help you overcome social anxiety:

1. Practice confident body language
2. Immerse yourself in social situations
3. Keep a record of your interactions
4. Say yes to things that make you uncomfortable
5. Surround yourself with high quality sociable friends
6. Meditate
7. Introspection
8. Record Yourself
9. Be open to everyone
10. Make plans and invite people

Let's take a look at each of these 10 tips and how they can help you overcome social anxiety and build the confidence to talk to anyone.

1. Practice confident body language

I also wrote an extensive list of confident body language and anxious body language to avoid in Social Confidence Mastery. I've never seen a detailed list that extensive anywhere else so please check it out if you want to improve your body language.

If you've never felt confident before you might not have much practice using confident body language. By practicing body language you get a feel for what it's like to actually be high status or at least accepted among others.

Research even proves that confident body language actually influences your physiology, making testosterone and serotonin increase and cortisol, the stress hormone, decrease.

Of course you can't rely only on acting out confident body language. It must be combined with actually doing other things confident people would do. Such as talking to new people.

With that said, it is still valuable to be aware of what confident body language looks like. You might be able to lie with your words but your body language almost always says exactly what you are feeling.

You can try to use some confident power poses, but if inside you feel terrified then it will be obvious to everyone around you. So don't pretend you are confident when you aren't. People sense that and it's really repulsive when we sense fake people.

Authenticity is always better.

Even if you have to admit you are feeling a little nervous because you don't often go to social events, most people will be understanding. Especially because most people have to deal with some level of social inhibitions. The will at least be able to respect and relate to your authenticity.

2. Immerse yourself in social interactions

People often don't like state changes. When you wake up, you might not feel like getting out of bed. When you are awake you might stay up late because you don't feel like sleeping. When you are social and having fun it's easier to move to the next interaction.

However if you haven't had a real conversation with another person for a few weeks then you might not feel ready to immerse yourself in daily social interactions.

It's completely natural to resist socializing if you haven't done so recently. You can start with some simple events where people will likely be very friendly and easy to talk to.

An easy option is searching for events in your area on a site such as Meetup.com. This site has activities for any kind of topic or activity you might be interested in. They have meet ups to play board games, practice languages, play sports, discuss books and current events, yoga, hiking trips and anything you can think of! You can even find self-improvement groups you can join for support in your confidence building efforts.

In my experience Meetup events are completely stress free. It's easy to talk to everyone attending as you are all there for a mutual purpose. Meetups are an easy choice for finding opportunities to socialize and develop your confidence.

Maybe you still have the fear inside before you arrive. Maybe you are worried people will judge your awkwardness. But that doesn't matter. The way it works is you get the courage after you do what you are afraid of. Not before.

Eventually you will get used to various social environments and you can go to bigger events and social venues by yourself.

In fact it may be much more beneficial for you to go out alone. Force yourself to engage the social environment without needing a friend by your side. When you are with a friend it's easy to focus on talking with each other instead of conversing with new people. It's a convenient excuse for avoiding the discomfort of new experiences. By going out alone you get to challenge yourself to meet new people and gain experiences that will empower you.

3. Keep a record of your interactions

Keeping a record of your experiences is a helpful reminder of your successes. No matter what you encounter, it is success. Acceptance is success. Even rejection is success because it's an opportunity to make yourself stronger.

Writing down your thoughts about social interaction helps you reflect on what you've learned and what you should do differently in the future.

You don't need to write down every detail of every interaction. You only need to spend about 10 minutes a day taking some notes on 1 or 2 interactions you had during the day.

Here are the key points you might write down:

1. What happened?
2. How did I feel?
3. How did I react?
4. How can I improve next time?

It may sound simple but this exercise is crucial to developing social awareness. By writing about your awkward, embarrassing, emotionally painful experiences you can be honest with yourself about their impact on you instead of hiding your pain and pretending you are flawless.

It also helps to reinforce helpful lessons.

It's a practice in honestly embracing reality.

Conversely, if you have endless positive experiences but never reflect on them you are also missing out on opportunities to learn and improve.

4. Say yes to things that make you uncomfortable

Only refuse something you know to be dangerous.

In most social situations fear is not proportionate to actual danger. If you see a cute stranger, feel the urge to say "hi," but the only reason you don't do it is that uncomfortable feeling in your gut scaring you out of it, then it is even more reason to do it.

Because you should prove to yourself it is completely safe.

The worse that could happen is they aren't in a social mood and walk away. Even if you get a rude reply, it doesn't take anything away from who you are. Talk to a few more people and you'll eventually find someone much friendlier to chat with.

The only thing preventing you from starting an enjoyable interaction in that scenario was fear. When the only reason you don't want to do something is because you're scared, then you should do it!

Here is an analogy which highlights how ridiculous this is. Pretend you are a child. You are very shy and don't want to go to a new school because you are worried you won't make friends. You are worried the teacher will yell at you. You cry and beg your parents to let you stay home. And they do let you stay home forever and never go to school. And every time you beg your parents to let you avoid social interaction they submit to your requests. You never need to buy something in a store, make phone calls, ask directions, or do anything that involves interacting with another human being. What kind of person do you think you would turn into?

Of course, you would most likely turn into an extremely timid person terrified of talking to anyone. Mostly because of lack of experience and the habit of avoiding experiences you assume to be scary. The more experiences you avoid the scarier you think people are.

In this scenario, do you think your parents did a good job of raising you? Didn't protecting you from potentially uncomfortable experiences do more harm than good? Sure you were able to avoid some embarrassing moments but at what cost? You are left with no social experience and never resolved that social anxiety. Eventually you were crushed under its weight.

Isn't a parent like that completely irresponsible? You could have learned so much if your parent had forced you to do the most emotionally painful choice. You would have gained numerous experiences that forced you to grow.

Hopefully you see the point of this analogy already. It's up to you to be your own parent and force yourself to make the best decisions for your growth especially when it's uncomfortable. When you allow yourself to chicken out of an opportunity to grow up you are only being irresponsible with your own life and happiness.

5. Surround yourself with high quality friends

Perhaps you have heard the idea that you are the average of the people you spend the most time with. The people around you definitely influence who you become. So it's important to be aware of the impact your friends have on you.

Some people say you should kick all the negative people out of your life and surround yourself with only positive people who support everything you say. But if people are only willing to give you positive feedback you are left unbalanced.

What you should really want are honest friends.

Some assume negative people are constantly complaining and whining and should be avoided to preserve positive emotions.

That is often true. Some people just have a nasty personality its best to avoid. But this doesn't mean all negativity should be ignored. Often your friends criticize you because they hope to see you succeed, not because they want to tear you down.

While criticism may on the surface appear negative, it can actually be very positive when the intention behind it is to help you.

This is why you should spend time with people who have different viewpoints from your own. When everyone around you is always confirming your biases that is also an impediment to growth.

It's possible you've never contemplated what kind of friend you'd like to have in your life.

Many friendships just form over a few conversations and it just seems to work out. These relationships are formed from the investments we make in each other. Unfortunately, you might end up with friends who take more value from you than they give back. You don't need to cut people out of your life if they have traits you admire. But you can still find more people who are exactly like what you want to become. You can find confident friends. You can find friends you want to learn from. You can find friends you would really enjoy spending time with.

6. Meditate

There are many proven benefits to mediation. Studies have shown that mediation can change the brain in ways that make you less prone to anxiety and stress.

What I really like about mediation is it allows me to ignore all the past and present nonsense of life. I can tune out all the distractions. I become present to the moment. At least that's my goal. Sometimes a certain topic will keep repeating in the mind. You don't need to control your thoughts. You just need to observe them. And ask yourself, "Why in the world did I think that?"

Meditation is also helpful to reigning in uncontrollable negative emotional reactions. For most people negative reactions are automatic. You've likely observed people going nuts over the smallest thing. I've seen people angrily shouting expletives for the pettiest reasons. Such as a fast food restaurant being out of an item they wanted. They lose their agency. They shout and swear. The world didn't fulfill their desires and they want revenge.

By quietly disconnecting from the petty disappointments of life we can calm the mind. With regular meditation the body gets a chance to take a break from negative thoughts that drain energy and the body's resources.

Let's imagine your body is a car. When you allow your emotions to take control of your behavior it's like letting the car drive itself. Where is the driver? You should be driving your car. You should be consciously choosing your thoughts and emotions. However this can be a challenge when we are stuck in the habit of letting the car drive itself. This means that if for example you are angry, that emotion will dictate your behavior. However, if you can maintain a calmer state of mind, you can still react appropriately without letting the negative emotions impede your judgement. With practice meditation can help alleviate emotional overreactions.

In 2010 an article in the Journal of Consulting and Clinical Psychology surveyed 39 studies of meditation based therapy on general social anxiety and other conditions, mostly mood related. The total sample of participants included 1140 people. In a majority of these studies people did experience relief from stress, anxiety, and related conditions with the help of regular meditation. The conclusion of this article was that meditation *"is a promising intervention for treating anxiety and mood problems in clinical populations."*

The science indicates meditation helps with anxiety, stress and social intelligence. It's connected to diminishing lonely negative thoughts. It's also a vital part of accepting the internal struggles that lead to social anxiety and unnecessary fear.

You don't need these thousands of studies to prove to you meditation has tangible benefits. You only need to try it to see for yourself. It takes an effort to start a regular mediation habit but eventually you will see results.

There are many established benefits to meditation:

- Enhances your emotional well-being
- Decreases anxiety and depression
- Improves resilience to pain and adversity
- Increases optimism
- Improves mood
- Increases mental strength and focus
- Improves memory
- Better creative thinking
- Helps you ignore distractions
- Improves immune system
- Reduces blood pressure
- Improves brain and heart disorders

If you feel resistance to the idea of meditation, please write a list of why you don't want to do it. If you are feeling too lazy to write a list, at least think about it for a moment. Why can't you spend 5 minutes a day alone with your thoughts? You must be able to find 5 minutes of time to yourself each day.

The more excuses you have for avoiding meditation the more you need it in your life! Because more excuses indicates you are addicted to external stimuli and are having trouble taking a break. It's ok to relax for a few minutes to an hour of very relaxing meditation. The world will still be there when you get back.

When you first start meditating it may in fact feel boring. You are just sitting there and nothing is happening.

But that is exactly the point.

You may have become addicted to always having something to do. Always having a phone in your hands, a computer on your lap, a song to listen to, or some other form of entertainment.

While enjoyable, these are distractions. When you can train yourself to resist these temptations, you will simultaneously train willpower and emotional control.

Even after people acknowledge how beneficial meditation is, why do they still refuse to develop this habit? The simple answer is they are already addicted to their daily routines. They dismiss meditation because they don't yet believe in the benefits.

Meditate daily for a month before you decide it's worthwhile or not. You don't need to take the word of regular meditators or the research backing up the benefits, you can simply try out meditation for yourself if you don't have a regular meditation habit yet.

Meditation would take away a chunk of time most people would rather spend on their cravings for other stimulation, such as TV, food, and internet browsing. Some say meditation is just a waste of time. But this is only because they have never practiced meditation themselves and haven't yet experienced the benefits.

For them, meditation has not yet been recognized as the reward it really is.

With meditation you have a chance to break free from your habits and emotions.

To get started you simply need to find your motivation for building this worthwhile habit.

There are many different kinds of meditation. In the most basic form you sit or lie down in a comfortable position, close your eyes, and pay attention to your thoughts. Don't try to control your thoughts, just let them go wherever they want and pay attention to what is happening.

This is the basic process of developing mindfulness. You don't need to memorize some complicated meditation techniques to experience the benefits of meditation. However when you realize the benefits of basic meditation it might be helpful for you to research more advanced meditation practices to help you on your journey of improving yourself.

Basic Meditation:

There are many different types of meditation. Each with variations that are supposed to help alleviate different burdens or help you improve in different ways.

There are many forms of meditation. Some are overly complicated. Some authors write a long list of 50 or more steps for what to imagine, feel, and how to breathe at which point in the meditation. I'm sure some of those forms of meditation with a long series of steps can in fact be very effective for their goals.

Go ahead and look for information on those types of meditations if they interest you. I like how having a series of steps during meditation such as breathing and visualizations can distract you from how much time is passing, which is great if you are still worried about being disconnected from your usual routine.

However you don't need to over contemplate it. Meditation is very simple and so here I want to provide some simple suggestions for how to benefit from usual meditation.

It's important to set regular times to your meditation practice each day as this helps you to associate that time with your meditation practice. As mentioned I recommend adding meditation to your morning and bedtime routines.

Commit to at least 5 minutes each time.

This will make it easy to remember. It can be relaxing to stretch first to loosen your muscles and tendons. If you can, find a place that you can devote to meditation, such as a certain chair or comfortable spot in a room. This will help you to associate this location with the relaxing states of meditation.

1. **Sit in a comfortable position.**
   (Unless you want to challenge yourself with an uncomfortable position, your choice.) Take a few slow deep breaths. Many recommend breathing through your nose if you can. Though it isn't necessary.

2. **Bring your attention to your body.**
   Pay attention to your senses. What do you feel? Slowly shift your attention from your feet up through the rest of your body. This is to transition your mind into a more relaxed state by first paying attention to how your body is sensing the world and how you are feeling.

3. **Observe your thoughts.**

Once you are relaxed you can move on to the next step. You don't need to try and control your thoughts. Some forms of meditation do however involve the practice of developing focus. During those forms of meditation you would imagine some shape or image and focus only on that for as long as possible. Whenever your mind is distracted you bring your thoughts back to the image you are focusing on. That is effective at developing focus and you may try if you like. However it is not necessary to experience the many benefits of meditation.

Simply being aware of your thoughts as your minds drifts is enough. When your mind wanders, just tell yourself its ok and come back to relaxing. There is no need to resist any thought or sensation. Just let it all happen.

Pay attention to your breathing. Breathe in, breathe out. Don't try to control it, just let it happen naturally.

Don't stress yourself out about not seeing results immediately. It can be tempting to dismiss meditation if you only try it once or twice. However enough people have experienced significant psychological shifts as a result of daily meditation within as short of time as a month that it is highly recommended.

Observe how simple yet effective meditation is. You don't need to make it any more complicated than you like. If you aren't meditating regularly yet you won't know what benefits you could be missing out on until you try.

Advanced Meditation

Meditation is easy.

You just sit down, close your eyes, and listen to your mind talk with itself. Pay attention to the thoughts and be curious about where the thoughts and feelings are coming from.

Your basic meditation sessions may last anywhere from 10 minutes to half an hour and then you come out of it at least a bit more relaxed and ready to tackle life's responsibilities.

But I want to share with you a more advanced form of meditation that can train you for reinterpreting pain and various frustrations in life especially when it comes to social anxiety and the fear of rejection.

But first, contemplate the following question for a moment. What would happen if you had a completely pain free life? Maybe you were born with that condition where your pain receptors don't work. Well that's a cool super power isn't it!? You can fall down, break bones, get punched in the face, and none of it will hurt!

There would be damage of course, and many accidents as you were sure of the effects of any action you take. But at least you won't be able to feel it.

Then one day, a doctor tells you, *"Hey buddy, we've developed a new treatment that can turn on all your dormant pain receptors! You would finally be able to feel pain!"*

You decide to give it a try. Of course it's successful. You tap the back of your hand gently on the wall to test out your new ability and think to yourself, **"wow, so this is pain."** But that wasn't a real test, your pain receptors haven't even been engaged yet. Then later you are cutting some vegetables and accidently cut your finger a little. You suddenly scream in agony. *"Oh shit I cut myself! I'm dying!"* You fall to the floor. Tears flowing out of your eyes as you can't control your reaction.

Pain wasn't a part of your reality before. In fact pain doesn't need to be part of our reality. We have the ability to feel pain because it prevents us from doing stupid things that would damage ourselves. The role of pain is usually to indicate to us when there is a problem.

It wasn't even a deep cut. Your finger is barely bleeding, but because you never felt pain before you have no reference for the level of pain you can actually endure.

This metaphor applies to every kind of discomfort. If you are focused on avoiding pain, then you are resisting the present moment.

Pain is resistance to your current situation. All discomfort is resistance to your current situation. So instead of resisting, you should accept the present moment. By accepting your situation, you no longer interpret it as painful, uncomfortable or annoying. It is that interpretation that makes it painful.

That is why in this form of meditation you sit completely still for at least one hour. Sit in a comfortable position and stay there. Don't move at all for as long as you can. See how long you can stand complete stillness before the aches and itches in your body prevent you from continuing.

If you feel an itch don't scratch it. Just accept the itch. You may be surprised to find that within a minute or two most itches will just disappear on their own.

If any part of your body begins to ache, resist the urge to change positions. Accept the feelings you feel. Though uncomfortable you will survive.

This kind of meditation teaches you to accept reality no matter how it is. In fact, it teaches you to reinterpret discomfort as not being uncomfortable at all. This trains you to accept adversity, annoyances and a bit of pain. This is the super power you should really want. It's so much better than the inability to feel pain at all.

So how long can you endure of this type of meditation? Most people seem to be barely able to endure 10 minutes. They are used to resisting discomfort and avoiding pain. It's a useful survival strategy. However it's often much more uncomfortable than it needs to be.

Most annoyances in your life don't need to affect your emotions as much as they do. So you are late for work? So what? Be late. It's just a job. So your boss yelled at you for being late? So what? Assure him you won't be late again, make an effort to be on time and move on with your life. Why does it need to stress you out?

There must be more examples like that in your life. Minor annoyances that you interpret as uncomfortable and constantly resistant. That resistance is what makes you feel negative emotions. Those negative emotions drain your body of nutrients essential to producing the neurotransmitters that provide positive emotions.

This translates to less fear of rejection and a more solid confidence in yourself as your emotions begin to come from yourself rather than other people.

How long can you endure this kind of meditation?

5 Minutes – Did you even try?

You give up easily when facing a challenge. You are easily frustrated when things don't go your way. You may lie to yourself and say you can sit here for an hour if you really wanted to, but the first time your nose really starts itching you are scratching hard. You might also tell yourself that one itch you scratched is a freebie and thus didn't count. So you refuse to start over.

10 Minutes - Average

Sometimes you give up on new things when you feel it doesn't suit you. But at least you give a real effort. You really wanted to meditate in complete stillness for an hour, and you managed to get past a few small itches. You can get through some challenges that other people whine about. However some big challenges require you to make a bigger effort to actually achieve success.

30 Minutes – Experienced Meditator

Maybe you haven't been meditating for years yet, but you may have been practicing meditation daily for at least 2 weeks. You are starting to realize you can stay calm in some situations that previously annoyed you. However your habits of resisting discomfort keep coming back. Eventually you will give up when the pain is too much.

1 hour – Yoda

You have more than a few weeks of meditation experience. You might be a bit neurotic about training yourself to resist pain. You are more honest with yourself than many people. You are able to overcome many difficulties but you can at least admit to yourself when something becomes too challenging for you. You also start to feel more energized no matter what discomfort is present in your life.

2 hours - Superman

If you can sit completely still and resist the urge to move at all for 2 hours then you are definitely starting to feel some changes happening within you. Any discomfort you feel in your chest may start to loosen up and you can actually feel this happening. You are becoming more sociable and tolerant of previously annoying nonsense. You have accomplished a few great things in your life, but there is much more you dream about accomplishing. Your challenges are numerous, so choose that ones you are more passionate about.

4 hours – Buddha

If you can do this for 4 hours you might be enlightened. You will definitely experience something. You will also find you are becoming much more positive than before.

8 hours – Master of the Universe

Congratulations. You may be in complete control of your emotions. Nothing bothers you. Luckily you can still behave appropriately depending on the situation since you are still a human being interacting with other people. But the discomforts that used to trouble you are seen for the events they really are.

I recommend trying this form of advanced meditation after you have been practicing regular mediation for at least 2 weeks. Though I'm not your boss so go ahead and test yourself to see how long you can last.

After you can handle normal meditation for 20 minutes a day then aiming for an hour of advanced meditation several times a week will likely benefit you. It is of course a habit that works best over time. The longer you have spent practicing the more benefit it gives you. The more you are able to accept the present moment without judging. But it takes time to cultivate these things as meditation rewires your brain. Meditation alone won't cure your social anxiety. You also need to take action and get yourself into social situations. With practice meditation will help you stay centered when you take action and resist the negative emotional reactions that tempt you to shy away from confidently expressing yourself.

7. Introspection

We learn from experience and mistakes. No matter how awkward or embarrassing, many of these experiences can become valuable lessons in self-improvement instead of sources of shame. People are terrified of experiences they don't need to be afraid of. A shy guy is scared to talk to new people. Not for any logical reason. He just has an unexplainable fear of approaching new people. When he does find an ounce of courage to start a conversation he might make awkward or needy statements. He might display weak body language. He might stutter and avoid eye contact. However these are all learning opportunities. The only real mistake would be in not learning from these experiences and making an effort to improve his social skills.

Unfortunately it's possible to pass up opportunities for growth if you never reflect on your experiences. Research indicates that thinking about what you've been through and asking yourself what it means and how to improve is usually prerequisite for learning. Think of it like this. There must have been times you've sat in a class taught by a teacher you considered boring. His lessons may have been very informative but if you only passively listened to what was taught in class you likely didn't remember much of the material. You might also have memories of a teacher you found entertaining or you were very interested in the subject of the class. In that instance, you would be actively thinking about the topic, you would be forming questions in your mind and actually learning something.

Life experience is the same way. You can choose to be a passive observer and never learn anything from what's been thrown at you, or you can learn how to anticipate it and dodge.

Reflecting on your life experiences takes you from passive observation to understanding. If you understand your mistake its more likely you will make a plan to resolve it. Otherwise you might keep making the same mistake.

When you are in a social situation at work, school, event or party focus on the moment. Meet some people and practice expressing yourself honestly. Afterwards ask yourself:

"What did I do well?"

"What can I improve?"

This helps you make incremental progress towards improving your ability to express yourself and overall confidence in social situations.

This next point may be uncomfortable to accept. Even more importantly, reflection forces you to challenge your assumptions about reality. You may be forced to face uncomfortable truths that you don't want to accept. For example, many socially inexperienced men love to complain that women are all superficial and only date handsome rich men. Some women may in fact be this way but there are plenty of exceptions to this. I've seen lots of short balding guys of average to little wealth attracting lots of stunning women through their confidence and social skills alone. But the socially inexperienced guy is blind to that reality. His confirmation bias only allows him to see the women dating the good looking guys. This way he can maintain this false concept as an excuse to avoid self-improvement.

But what would happen if he had a more open mind? What if when faced with immense evidence to the contrary of his view he asked himself it was really ALWAYS true? Perhaps he would be open to the possibility that it was his social skills that were the major hindrance to his failure to find a girlfriend. Perhaps he would eventually give up on the negative belief that, "Women hate me because I'm ugly!" Even if you are ugly, I think women hate you because your negative personality makes people uncomfortable not the excuses you tell yourself to avoid confronting your flaws.

The point is to be open to questioning your ideas of the world. This opens you up to many possibilities.

In the scenario above the man with a pessimistic view of his dating life could realize he has the potential to develop his social skills and share life with some incredible people if he only believed it were possible instead of assuming nobody would ever want to socialize with him because of his below average appearance.

It's not only helpful to reflect on your mistakes.

It's also beneficial to reflect on your achievements and remind yourself what you've done well in social situations.

Even when you do make mistakes you can frame it very positively as a learning opportunity.

8. Record yourself.

If you've never video recorded yourself it can be uncomfortable at first to see and hear yourself. You may realize you have some bad habits you weren't aware of. If you can, record yourself talking with another person.

When you watch it pay attention to the volume and tone of your voice, eye contact, posture. Listen for any odd verbal ticks or indications of nervousness. Ask yourself why you felt that way in that moment.

This exercise forces you to confront nervous body language and bad habits that usually can be corrected with practice.

Record yourself in this manner several times over a few months and you will likely see a difference in your ability to express yourself more confidently.

9. Be open to everyone

Most people you meet won't become your friend. That doesn't mean you need to ignore potential value they could add to your life and that you could add to theirs.

In some venues you will notice needy individuals who are only interested in socializing with certain people. If it is at a night club it may be a needy guy who only talks to women and refuses to befriend her male friends and toxically sees them as "obstacles." Or if it is a more formal setting people might only be interested in meeting wealthy individuals with social status and completely ignore the penniless entrepreneur even though he is a highly interesting man with a lot of value to offer.

As you can see, this is a very selfish, needy, value taking frame of mind. When you have a goal it can be tempting to focus only on the people that can help you achieve it and ignore all the other opportunities for human connection. But you are missing out. In fact, you don't know what opportunities you could be missing out on if you act in such a selfish way. The guy in the night club could have talked to some overweight ladies, and then attractive girls could have seen him having fun and socializing with anyone, not just focused on extracting a target. Providing value is very attractive. Or maybe those overweight ladies had some cute friends. The snobs at the formal get together lost an opportunity to invest in the entrepreneur who later became a billionaire. You don't know what opportunities you are missing by being so closed minded and focused on exactly what you want.

Real social confidence should involve being willing to interact with anyone. It doesn't mean you always need to though.

Some people just can't relax and are intimidated by stress free people with social skills. However in most social situations it should be acceptable to interact with most people. In fact, it should also be enjoyable.

If you limit the kinds of people you interact with it will likely lead to frustration. Because that limitation you place on yourself causes unnecessary stress.

You may think you aren't cool enough to talk to an interesting person you'd like to meet. But you'll never know if they are willing to talk to you or not unless you try. Conversely you may think someone isn't interesting enough to talk to.

Many people only seem boring on the surface. Even sufferers of social anxiety. But once you get them relaxed and comfortable they can willingly share their humor and individuality.

Being open to new people, ideas, and experiences expands your intellectual capacity. Instead of only talking to people who look and think like you it can be an intriguing experience to interact with people with vastly different world views than your own.

One fear in social situations is that you might have an opinion or belief that conflicts with the person you are talking to. This could result in an uncomfortable confrontation in which the other person says you are wrong or insults you for your belief. Instead of fearing that scenario learn to embrace it. Be happy when it happens. Maybe you and the other person involved have something to teach each other.

Being open to others without limitations diminishes prejudices, makes you more optimistic, and has been shown to significantly decrease stress. This is because you aren't constantly afraid people will threaten you with their different way of thinking or living.

Possibly the most significant benefit to openness to everyone is that you gain incredibly valuable social experience. Instead of worrying what to do in a variety of situations you will know exactly what to do because you've already been in that situation many times before. Whether is a pleasurable or annoying situation you will already be prepared to handle it.

You could read 100 amazing books about developing confidence and not understand how to do it. However when you openly embrace and handle an immense variety of social situations it will fundamentally change you.

After interacting with people from a wide range of backgrounds and temperaments you won't be as scared of social situations as before. If you reflect on these experiences you will realize they are even more valuable than any book could ever articulate to you. That solid understanding based on actual experience is essential to developing genuine confidence.

10. Make plans and invite people

When you've started going to more social events, reflecting on your experiences, and meeting people you are interested in getting to know better it may be time to turn your new acquaintances into friends or more.

Socially successful people don't only sit and wait for invitations to hang out. They make plans and carve reality to their liking.

Think of an activity you would genuinely like to do with a few new friends.

Some examples:
- Drinking / clubbing
- Karaoke
- Paintball
- Beach volleyball
- Surfing
- Any sport
- Billiards
- Dinner at a theme restaurant
- Potluck dinner party at your house
- Picnic
- Board games
- Video games

- Hiking
- Biking
- Start a group on meetup.com and host meetups

It doesn't need to be elaborate. It could simply be dinner with a few of your new friends. You can have a great conversation and if things are going well have a plan for where to invite people after the meal.

When you start organizing events such as this people see you as a leader and they will start asking you to hang out. They will want to be invited to the next fun get together you organize. As long as people are having fun and enjoy your company it should be easy to gradually develop a regular group of people you can hang out with anytime. This shouldn't be much of an issue if you have been following a majority of the advice in this book for at least a few weeks.

Taking responsibility for social situations will be a huge boost to your confidence in social situations as well. Instead of worrying about what other people think of you, it's more likely your new acquaintances will be anxious about impressing you. After all, they want to hang out with you and meet your other interesting friends.

Obviously that is the ideal and life isn't always that simple. You might be the most sociable and fun person but it's difficult to make connections with interesting people you meet because they are too busy with their own plans. However this is no excuse to dismiss taking action in this area of your life. Maybe the people you invite will already have plans. Interesting people often have busy social lives already.

That doesn't mean they are completely uninterested in hanging out with you. They may legitimately be busy. So spend a few weeks busy with your own plans. Have fun, meet and date new people, go on more adventures, read more books, live the life you want to live. And then the next time you invite someone to hangout it might be easier.

Should You Treat Social Anxiety With Antidepressants?

I have mixed feelings about this topic because I prefer to be completely self-reliant to overcome fears and build confidence.

I have also seen a lot of people who are unfortunately dependent on antidepressants in order to socialize at all. From observation, they often still suffer from a lot of negative thoughts, especially when off of their medication. They are usually convinced that prescribed medication is the ONLY way they can behave like a normal human being. I understand why they think that way though. It's because it's their interpretation of what they've experienced.

On the other hand, there are people with severe social anxiety who would definitely benefit from using antidepressants. Because of anxiety, they have been unable to develop social skills. Even if they tried to face their social fears they would worry too much about embarrassing themselves.

People who've sunk too deep into the pit of anxiety may feel it's impossible to escape. Perhaps they could get some benefit from moderate use of anti-anxiety medication.

At least they would be able to get some reference experiences for what social confidence actually looks and feels like.

They would actually be able to believe they are capable of expressing themselves to others without stuttering or running away in fear.

So if you think antidepressants or other antianxiety medication might be useful training wheels for gaining real confidence then visit a qualified, trustworthy psychiatrist who can assist you in your goals. Taking medication that alters your brain is something you should do with maturity and intelligence. Be sure you use such items wisely if you feel it's necessary.

How to Deal with Physical Symptoms of Anxiety

Later we will discuss managing the psychological discomfort of social anxiety. In this chapter we will discuss ways to manage its external symptoms.

Some of these symptoms can include sweating, blushing, stuttering, shaky hands and more.

Many social anxiety suffers experience increased breathing when their anxiety is triggered. This reaction is part of the fight, flight or freeze response. Also known as the stress response. Your body is preparing for danger because you've interpreted something to be dangerous.

Your body is getting ready to kick ass, run or hide. As a result, you start breathing quickly in short shallow breaths. This is because your body now demands an increase of oxygen in the blood, muscles and brain. Your interpretation of experiencing danger of course triggers a variety of biological reactions that are useful when you are about to handle conflict, but can have detrimental effects on your health when you constantly interpret harmless situations as life threatening.

If your body doesn't do anything with that increased oxygen it creates an imbalance in the oxygen to carbon dioxide ration in the body. So more oxygen and less CO_2.

You might get light headed, feel dizzy, even tingling sensations with enough oxygen. The flight or fight response prepares your body for physical action! This means your body is focused on escaping or defeating the danger. Rational parts of your brain shut down to conserve energy and focus on your survival. This is why it may seem like you are completely incapable of talking to anyone without sounding like an idiot when you are nervous.

To manage these symptoms you can practice Controlled Breathing.

Stress response breathing is short and shallow. Since it heavily increases the amount of oxygen, and in fact makes you feel even more nervous, it can be helpful to intentionally take deep breathes in and then exhaling slowly.

This helps you to gain control over your breathing. Remember this: Your thoughts influence your biology. Such as thinking people are dangerous and you unnecessarily get nervous. But the opposite is also true. If you are breathing as if you are relaxed, it can actually make you feel less stressed.

Inhale as deeply as possible.

Slowly exhale and pay attention to your breathing.

This helps to minimize your stress response and consequently other related symptoms.

Before you try using this technique in actual social situations, you can try practicing it on your own.

Begin by imagining a social scenario that scares you. Practice mentally rehearsing a stress free response to that situation.

Pay attention to how fast you breathe in and own. Many medical professionals recommend that breathing in and out with your nose is healthier so try it if you can.

Imagine as many details as possible. And when you get to the moment that usually frightens you, remember to take a deep breath in and pay attention to your slow exhale out.

Doing this for 5 minutes every day can help you to mentally and physically prepare for encountering social situations that trigger your anxiety.

How to Stop Avoiding Social Situations

As we've established, facing your fears is one of the most important parts of overcoming them.

People inevitably use lots of ridiculous excuses to avoid facing situations that make them uncomfortable. But avoidance won't resolve your problems. They fear will persist.

The more you avoid the more anxiety you will feel. The more you avoid the more you retard your already limited social skills.

How often have you been invited to a social event but made up some excuse to avoid going? It's ok if you have a legitimate reason. And it's understandable for normal people to occasionally not feel like socializing. But if you are honest with yourself you will know if you avoid social situations out of fear.

You must acknowledge your responsibility for your social anxiety, confidence, and social status. There is no secret trick that will make you permanently fearless. To build confidence you must gain reference experiences that convince you of what you are capable of.

Fear only exists before you take action. You might be nervous before doing anything you haven't done before. Learning to drive, diving from a high board, learning a new skill, public speaking or going to a new place, or event.

Nervousness often comes from the fact you are completely unaware of how to behave to gain acceptance from others. You don't know what rules to follow or actions to avoid. You don't know if the people in the new environment will be accepting or intimidating.
It's the fear of the unknown.

But you must have had experiences when you were very nervous before trying something new, but then during and after the experience realized it wasn't so bad.

Try to think of a few experiences like that.

Except for some over exaggerated emotional baggage from past memories you might be carrying with you, social situations are exactly the same.

You will usually be most nervous before any socializing even begins. You might be scared to start a new conversation because you could be ignored, or rejected. But then will happily relax when this new person gives a friendly reaction and you can actually have a good talk.

Therefore, it should be obvious that social anxiety is often an irrational fear that comes from an excessively negative imagination.

You've trained yourself to think like that. Every time you've considered starting a conversation with a stranger you worry about all sorts of impossible consequences.

It's time to start training yourself to think more positively. Start imagining the best possible reaction you could get. And accept it. Such as everyone loves talking to you, or whatever you hope to get from socializing.

Then imagine the worst possible reaction and multiply it by 10. Such as people insulting you, criticizing you, rudely and loudly accusing you of all sorts of evil deeds.

And then accept that obviously ridiculous situation. Imagine it happens and you are completely okay with it. So someone insulted you. So what? You are still alive. Their rude words weren't true anyway.

Practice accepting these highly unlikely scenarios and it will help you accept the much more likely results you will probably get. In most social situations the most common outcome is you'll get a polite, friendly, short interaction. The worst possible reaction would be someone ignoring you. Maybe they are in a hurry. Maybe they are dealing with their own social anxiety issues.

When you do this mental exercise the intent should be to convince yourself that nothing bad will happen to you when socializing. Even if you do encounter rude people, try to reframe those experiences as positive. As mentioned before, they are experiences that help you build real confidence. A little trauma makes you stronger.

You don't need to resolve all your social anxiety immediately.

Don't hope one day of positive interactions can cure you of shyness for life.

It will take time to reverse the habits of social anxiety you've created for yourself.

With practice, you build confidence. I know you might wish you could magically turn off the fear. Especially because you know how irrational it actually is. But there is no better alternative than to face your fears, accept them, and accept yourself.

Imagine after several months of facing your fears, what kind of person will you become? How about after just 2 more years? And 10 more years? You likely could become a much more confident person if you invested in behavior that built your confidence. If however you keep investing in social avoidance, you will only get more scared of interacting with people and it will only hurt your life.

It will be scary to take any risk. You won't want to find new jobs, or experience anything new if your social anxiety is severe enough.

You should also start with the least anxiety inducing social fears first.

If you want a detailed plan for facing increasingly difficult fears I've outlined it in my FREE BOOK, How to Overcome Fear.

Go to www.evolvetowin.com to get your FREE copy now.

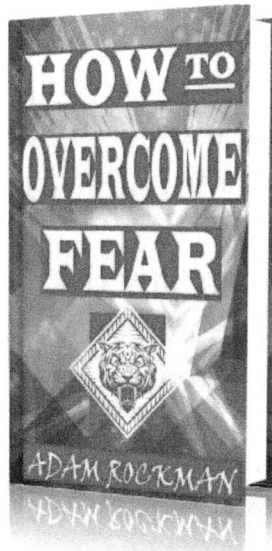

It explains in detail how to maintain motivation and enjoy the process of building more confidence in any situation. I'm giving book away for free because I've seen it help dozens of people just like you permanently overcome social anxiety.

10 More Tips for Social Confidence

Here are 10 More Tips for facing your fears and overcoming social anxiety so you can start to feel more confident talking to anyone.

1. **Mentally prepare for your worst fears.**
   We've already discussed mentally rehearsing for the worst case scenario and combining that with deep breathing to help you relax. When you spend your life avoiding social interactions you leave yourself incredibly unprepared for when uncomfortable situations inevitably happen. You won't know how to cope with embarrassment, being caught in a lie, intimidated, threatened, criticized, or any number of things that WILL happen to you.

   You can't pretend your life is perfect by avoiding the situations that frighten you. Eventually uncomfortable situations will that arise that force you to confront the fact you are seriously under prepared. This means, you must come up with a plan for accepting and handling any uncomfortable social situation that may arise.

2. Stay positive

Don't let setbacks make you worry too much. Just because one person isn't interested in talking to you doesn't mean the whole world hates you. Keep interacting with people and your confidence will increase and you will inevitably meet people you can connect with. The function of worry is to prevent action. It's meant to keep you out of trouble and help you survive. But survival alone isn't living or thriving. Only worry when it's absolutely necessary. By staying positive you open yourself up to more receiving more value and success in your life.

3. Sleep Well

You'll find this tip in many self-help books because it does effectively help with many conditions. Although obvious, lots of people neglect quality sleep and stay up late instead of establishing a regular sleeping schedule. Your body is like a clock. Eating and sleeping at regular times keeps it on the right time.

Lack of quality sleep clearly increases anxiety. Also, it makes it difficult to think clearly and you know you know you are more likely to talk like an idiot or not know what to say when your mind can barely function.

4. **Ask a Friend to Face Fears With You**
I think it's best if you do all your fear facing challenges on your own. It will help you learn self-reliance. However, I have to admit it can be very fun to face fears with friends who also have similar anxieties to your own.

The caveat however is you should still be will willing to face social fears completely on your own and without an audience to praise your efforts when you succeed.

5. **Don't Stick to People you are Comfortable With**
When you go to social events, don't just hang out with the one person you know. It's a sign you aren't comfortable talking to other people. Also, don't glue yourself to the first person you talk to. You might worry ending the interaction means you'll have nobody to talk to. Feel that

fear and embrace it. Stop worrying if you can't find the next person to have a fun chat with.

6. **Stop Relying on External Validation**

External validation means you are happy and feel confident every time someone praises or acknowledges you. Are you only happy when people are smiling at you and accepting your presence? Does your happiness really depend on what others think of you? If yes then that is extremely weak. By practicing internal validation, you can choose to be as happy and confident as you want to be. Your emotions are always in your control. However, that doesn't make it easy.

You may be able to say the words, "I want to be confident." But you won't be able to believe it because too much trauma and too many anxious memories in your life are convincing you that's impossible. You have to accept that trauma and those memories. And then you have to face your fears so you can actually start believing you are confident.

7. Join Groups on Meetup.com and Attend Events

Meetup.com is an awesome website. You can find groups for any kind of interest, topic or hobby. There are sports groups, entrepreneur groups, book clubs, language exchanges, and various parties for making new friends. Anything you might be interested in will have a relevant group in your area.

If you are serious about overcoming social anxiety and making friends then this is a must. If you are a university student there will likely be some clubs and events available that would interest you too. Commit to going to at least 1 social event a week.

8. Get Regular Exercise

Exercise is another common essential to life that you'll hear everyone reminding you to include in your daily routine. Going to the gym, or for a run is proven to reduce stress hormones such as cortisol and increase the hormones that produce positive emotions. Regular exercise improves your health and decreases anxiety.

9. Practice Self-Acceptance

Self-acceptance means you accept the undesirable parts of yourself. There may be emotions, desires and thoughts you suppress for various reasons. In order to grow you must accept the darker parts of yourself. When you are embarrassed, show yourself compassion rather than beating yourself up about it.

And finally number 10:

Lean in To Your Fears

In new social situations you will encounter crucial moments in   which you must decide to either run away or accept the fear and take action anyway.

Your automatic routine may be to avoid saying or doing anything that could be rejected by others. Your desire for approval only hurts your chances of gaining it.

Instead, say exactly what you want to say. Do what you want to do. At first this will be challenging because you aren't used to it. It's like trying to lift a weight with a muscle you've never exercised before. It's going to be tough, but eventually you get stronger.

Try to find a way to enjoy this process of building your mental strength. I do this by realizing how much every interaction adds to my life experience and ability to handle future situations.

FREE BONUS CHAPTER

As an extra surprise, I want to give you this free bonus chapter from my book,

Social Confidence Mastery:

How to Eliminate Social Anxiety, Insecurities, Shyness, and the Fear of Rejection.

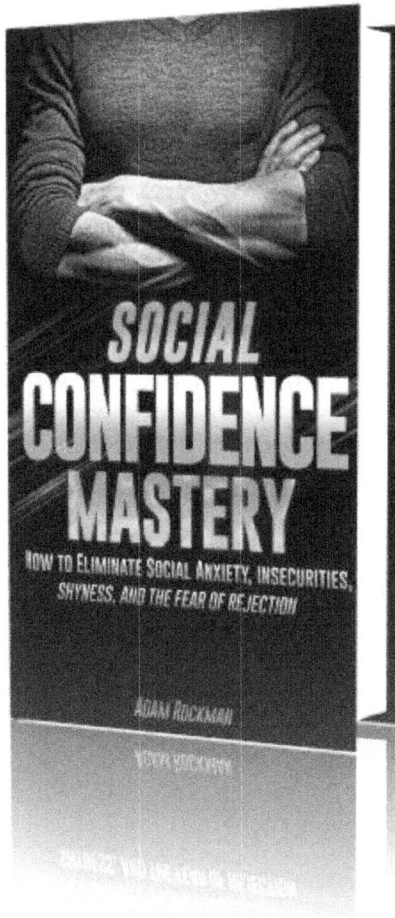

Social Confidence Mastery is over 300 pages of the best advice you will ever find for beating social anxiety AND building social confidence. It is a complete method because it teaches you how to turn your inner pain into strength, shows you exactly how the mind of socially confident people works, and how to actually speak and behave confidently in social situations.

If you want to know how to be respected, admired, and liked by as many people as possible and fearlessly express yourself in every situation then you must read Social Confidence Mastery. I only mention it in this book because If you like the advice you are reading here I know you will get even more value out of SCM. Please enjoy the following free chapter and I hope it helps you in your journey of overcoming social anxiety.

Free Bonus Chapter from

Social Confidence Mastery:

How to Overcome Social Anxiety

"Man is not worried by real problems so much as by his imagined anxieties about real problems."

— **Epictetus**

When we examine our disowned traits we look deep inside ourselves to see the roots of our fearful behavior and attempt to balance incongruities. Now we look at the external behaviors our fear of social situations manifest.

The spectrum of social anxiety can begin at mild shyness and go all the way to severe Avoidant Personality Disorder. No matter how extreme, social anxiety connects to fears of being observed, judged, embarrassed, or rejected.

How to love all social interactions

Talking with people is inevitable. People will randomly say annoying things to you. People will suddenly ask personal questions you don't want to answer. You'll need to attend social events. People will intimidate you. And obviously there are many interactions required in our daily lives to ensure everyone's survival. If you have to do it, you might as well find a way to enjoy it. At the very least you can accept these inevitabilities. The more you resist them the more you will avoid situations required to develop maturity and confidence.

Shyness often depends on who you are talking to, your role, the ages of people involved and other factors you might not even be consciously aware of.

To help you overcome the specific fears that trigger your own social anxiety, take a moment to answer the following questions:

1. Who triggers your social anxiety?

   - Coworkers
   - Your boss / manager
   - Acquaintances
   - Strangers
   - Friends
   - Authority figures such as police, doctor, employer etc.
   - Family members
   - People you would like to date
   - People who intimidate you
   - People physically larger than you
   - People who never smile
   - People who dress differently than you (more professional/ more fashionable etc.)
   - People who seem more successful than you
   - People you want to impress
   - One person
   - A group of people

- Neighbors
- Salespeople
- Other:_____

1. When talking to people, what triggers anxiety for you?

- Starting a conversation
- Ending a conversation
- Sharing personal information
- Superficial small talk (weather, news, etc.)
- Not knowing what to say
- Expressing your honest opinion, especially when it conflicts with what the other person said.
- Inviting someone to a date
- Speaking on the phone
- Asking for help
- Trying to impress others
- Making a suggestion (Where to eat, what to do etc.)
- Waiting for a positive reaction (smile, asking follow up question etc.)
- Asking boring questions you don't even really want to ask to keep the conversation going

- Making a request
- Disagreeing
- Expressing anger or dissatisfaction
- Other:_____

Looking at your answers to these two questions you can have a clear image of what specific people and actions trigger your social anxiety. Write these down so you can develop awareness of the situations you should work on. The situations and individuals to trigger your fear response will be unique to your own life experience. Some people may dread boring small talk with coworkers but have zero fear of starting conversations with beautiful strangers. Others might be socially fearless with coworkers and most people but stutter and shake nervously when they try to talk to someone they are romantically interested in.

Judgement Fear

If starting conversations still seems terrifying, there may be less obvious fears you should first address. Such as the fear of being observed and judged by others. If you are afraid of any of the following then make a note of it in your progress journal:

- Waiting in line
- Making eye contact with strangers
- Public transportation
- Eating in front of others
- Drinking in front of others
- Reading in front of others
- Writing in front of others
- Talking on the phone in public
- Using a crowded elevator
- Exercising in front of others
- Doing work that involves being observed by others

Performance anxiety

The fear of being judged can apply to any situation. Performance anxiety is a bit higher pressure as it can involve the risk of messing up. Everyone is paying attention to you and it's your turn to deliver what they expect. It's common to feel judged in these situations if you haven't practiced them.

What performance situations trigger your anxiety?

- Public speaking
- Giving a Presentation, speech, demonstration etc.
- Dancing in public
- Performing a skill you can do well if practiced alone but often fail at in public because of anxiety
- Taking a test
- Introducing yourself to a group of people
- Asking a question at a meeting
- Singing in front of others
- Being interviewed
- Asking questions / speaking when other people will overhear what you say
- Acting
- Sports competition

- Playing a game
- Playing a musical instrument
- Recording a video of yourself
- Counting money/change
- Making a complaint
- Artistic performance in public
- Talking to customers
- Cooperating on a group project
- Other _____

As you can see there are 3 distinct types of situations that can trigger social anxiety. Examine how conversation anxiety, general fear of being judged, and performance anxiety are problematic in your life.

Choose the 5 most anxiety inducing social situations.

Example:

1. Starting conversations with strangers
2. Sharing personal information
3. First dates
4. Public speaking
5. Not knowing what to say

The following questions and exercises will help you examine why these situations cause you so much unnecessary anxiety and help you think of ways to overcome them.

Let's now look at several key factors involved in causing you problems in these areas.

The Comfort Zone

To survive we obviously need safety. Psychologists agree that social anxiety likely has its utility in helping people survive. After all, if everyone was super confident they'd all take dangerous risks until our species was extinct. Fear and avoidance of danger is therefore completely natural. We instinctually find a comfort zone and protect it like an eagle protecting her nest. The size of the comfort zone of course depends on the person. Just because yours may be very small now doesn't mean it always needs to be.

When you establish your comfort zone anytime you reach its edge anxiety causes you to resist and pull away.

You will naturally develop habits that keep you feeling safe. Examples of these comfort zone habits are always letting friends order for you when you go to restaurants because you are afraid to speak to the waitress, or always staying with your friend when you go to a party because you are afraid to be alone.

Many people strictly avoid any social situation that could cause even the hint of anxiety. It may seem like a genius plan to avoid talking to cute strangers in order to avoid rejection but you would only be missing out on opportunities to develop social skills and reestablish the limits of your comfort zone. Living like this is not living at all.

Every opportunity you avoid, invitation you turn down shrinks the edge of the comfort zone. Insist on this type of behavior and you risk developing avoidant personality disorder and being terrified of even leaving your home.

Think of social situations you have avoided. What was the negative impact of this avoidance?

For example, you might want to go to some parties to make new friends, but you constantly cancel your plans to do this. The negative impact could be you continue to feel lonely, bored, and depressed.

Maybe you were tasked with giving a speech at work. You practiced, but still felt too scared to perform. You pretend you are sick and cancel it. You missed an opportunity to develop your public speaking skills, confidence, and to convince your boss you are responsible and worthy of a promotion. Try to use the 5 situations you have already written down if you can.

Socially anxious people are often ashamed of themselves. This inadequacy comes out in shy, self-conscious behavior. Such as avoiding eye contact, stuttering, speaking too quietly, etc. To hide both this shame and its symptoms they will adopt sneaky behaviors.

Be honest with yourself and you might realize you are guilty of some of these yourself. Here are some of the typical behaviors:

- *In conversation:* Asking lots of questions to avoid talking about yourself. Speaking quickly to say as much as possible without being interrupted. Fear of silence. Pauses in conversation make them feel anxious and they rush to fill it with something. Preparing topics instead of spontaneous conversation.

- *To hide anxiety:* wearing makeup, especially too much is often a sign someone isn't confident in their appearance. Holding a glass in front of the chest. Wearing an extra layer of clothes to hide nervous sweating.

- *In Social events:* Never leaving your friend's side. Staring at your phone pretending you have something important to do.

- *In Public:* Staring at your phone, avoiding eye contact, keeping distance between yourself and others, always getting out of everyone's way.

- *Disagreement avoidance:* Always agreeing, smiling, never complaining, and never revealing a conflicting opinion.

- *Attention avoidance:* Sitting in the back of a room, remaining as quiet as possible, begrudgingly doing whatever task you have been assigned without complaint.

- *Dating:* Always agreeing with everything your date says. Pretending to be impressed with things that might not even deserve it. Excessive complimenting instead of playful teasing.

If you are guilty of some of these don't worry. If you look for them you will see this type of anxiety avoidance is very common. And at least people engaging in these behaviors are trying to socialize even if they do so with this fear induced crutch.

However these behaviors still limit your ability to build real social connections and enjoy life. It's like you are a bird and you've been pushed out of the nest by big momma eagle. Instead of soaring away into the stratosphere you are clinging to the branch of these anxiety avoidance behaviors. If you only let go you could realize you actually have a pair of wings and already know how to fly instinctually. It's only the fear of flying that prevents you from actually doing it.

Take a moment to recognize your own anxiety avoidance behaviors. Be honest with yourself about why you do these things.

You might feel relief when you successfully avoid what you perceive to be a potentially anxiety inducing situation. But seriously ask yourself:

What are you giving up for that relief?

Write down at least one of these behaviors for each of your 5 most anxiety inducing situations.

Example:

Anxiety trigger: First dates

Anxiety avoidance behavior in this situation: Planning a list of questions before the date to avoid awkward silence triggering anxiety.

Negative impact of this behavior: Remaining fearful of spontaneous conversation and silent tension. Reinforces lack of confidence in your social skills.

List as many of these avoidance behaviors for each of your feared situations as possible. Follow this by contemplating and writing down the negative impact these behaviors have on your life. This will help you understand the real cost of avoidance.

Observe your Anxiety

Notice which situations make you worry about embarrassing yourself.

Focusing on the risk of encountering anxiety inducing situations will only intensify your negative feelings and the impulse to engage in avoidant behaviors will increase.

Logically you may realize the person looking at you is not likely to approach or speak to you. However you still feel an urge to avoid eye contact and run away.

Now that you are aware of which fears and behaviors are feeding your lack of social success you can devise a plan to transform these fears and expand your comfort zone. These behaviors hurt you much more than they help you. It's important to see that. If you focus on the benefits of changing these avoidant behaviors you will be much more likely to develop more beneficial habits.

How to change these bad habits

Every time you tighten your grip on the branch of avoidant behavior you reinforce negative thoughts of inadequacy, and lose opportunities to develop confidence. These processes usually occur subconsciously. But now that you are aware of them you can either take responsibility for your actions or feel even more like a loser because you know it's possible to change if you tried.

Giving up now would be like Neo choosing the red pill in the Matrix, realizing the truth of reality, getting scared and then pretending to go back to his blue pill existence in the make believe computer simulation. He might be able to lie to himself that it's more comfortable this way, but he is only hiding from reality and denying the truth.

Replacing avoidant behaviors with more confident ones isn't as easy as taking a magic pill that opens your eyes to reality. But it can similarly lead you to liberating realizations.

Let's examine how habits are formed and take advantage of this process to build more confident habits. Habits are basically formed in 3 steps:

1. **Trigger**: Outside event triggers social anxiety. Such as starting a conversation, someone suddenly asking you a question, or making a phone call

2. **Reaction:** The avoidant behavior that comes with the anxious response. Such as cancelling invitations, speaking too quietly, and running away from social situations.

3. **Reward:** The feeling of relief you get from the avoidant behavior.

You should already realize by now that the "reward" of relief you get from avoidant behavior should be viewed as negative and detrimental to your confidence. Now that you are aware of you can take responsibility for your reactions to them. You will feel the urge to do your usual avoidance behavior but that is exactly when you should adopt a new more positive reaction.

For example, if every time coworkers ask you questions you feel anxious and react by avoiding eye contact, speaking very little and then exiting the conversation as quickly as possible you can make a conscious effort to change this reaction to more eye contact, asking questions back to your coworkers, and staying in the conversation as long as possible. At first this may feel awkward because you aren't chasing the reward of relief in your usual avoidant way. However you can still convince yourself that these new behaviors are even more rewarding.

To make this even more effective you can use consistent rewarding behavior every time you react more confidently than usual. Such as eating a piece of chocolate or something similar.

Eventually you will form new habits that looks closer to this:

1. **Trigger:** Starting conversations with new people.

2. **Reaction:** The avoidant reaction might be to think of excuses to avoid speaking to someone. "They look busy." "I don't look cool enough today" etc. And then give up on socializing. Replace this reaction with always saying something to new people. At least "Hi" and a follow up statement or question is enough. You don't need people to give you an amazing reaction.

3. **Reward:** relief from realization it's acceptable and even enjoyable to start conversations with new people, eating a piece of chocolate, or something else you enjoy.

The new reactions will eventually become your usual response to these triggers. Every time you react appropriately you reinforce positive habits that help you develop both inner and outer confidence. You will be more comfortable in these social situations and more capable of interacting with others.

I hope this free bonus chapter from Social Confidence Mastery has been helpful to you.

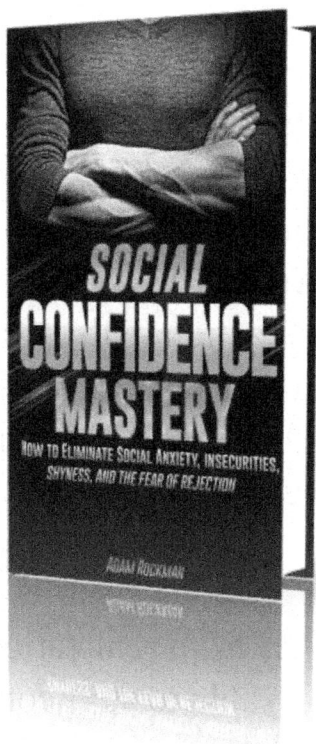

If you are serious about overcoming social anxiety then I highly recommend you read Social Confidence Mastery next. It not only includes a detailed encyclopedia of confidence building techniques, but also teaches you confident social skills for use in any situation.

Thanks for Reading!

I hope this book has provided inspiration to face your fears and develop social confidence.

I want to know about your efforts to Overcome Social Anxiety. In your Amazon review let me know if you think this information will help you. If you think some important part of overcoming social anxiety is missing, let me know and I will try to include it in the next edition.

Thanks again and I wish you sincere success with all your goals.

If you haven't yet received your free bonus book get it at   www.EvolveToWin.com

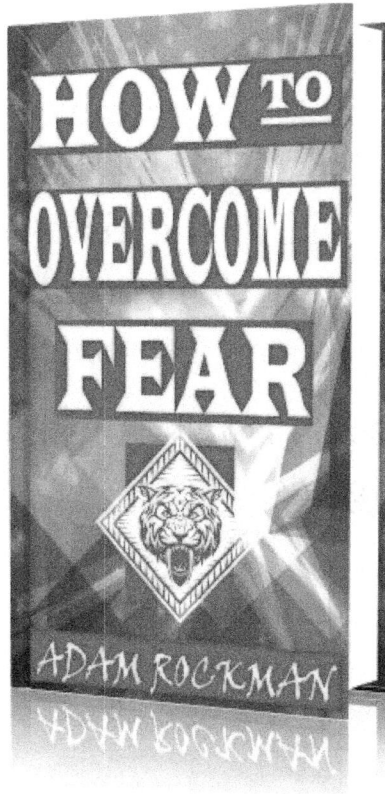

OTHER BOOKS BY THE AUTHOR

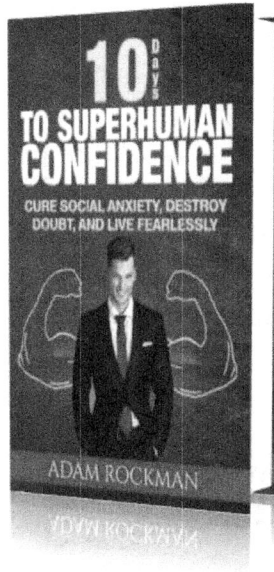

10 Days to Superhuman Confidence: Cure Social Anxiety, Destroy Doubt, and Live Fearlessly

"It's like the author was in my head and knew what has always been holding me back. I've wasted too much time trying to please everyone when I should first satisfy my own needs and goals to build my confidence"

— James Coney, Reader

OTHER BOOKS BY THE AUTHOR

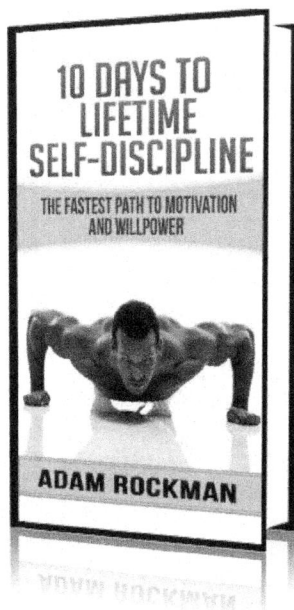

10 Days to Lifetime Self-Discipline: The Fastest Path to Motivation and Willpower

"Procrastination has always been my problem. After reading this book, I forced myself to go to the gym. I bought an annual membership for a year and feel the power to be able to beat my fat belly."

— Vasiliy

OTHER BOOKS BY THE AUTHOR

I Don't Fucking Care! : How to Stop Caring What People Think About You

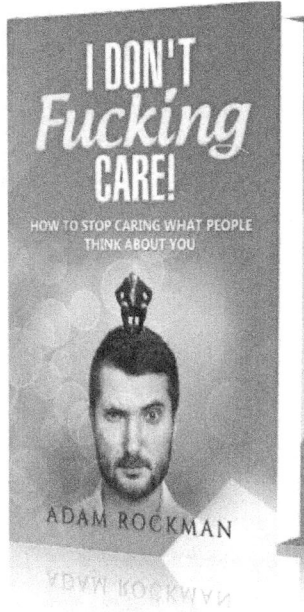

"This is the perfect book for me. I used to be very conscious of what other people think of me that I don't usually speak my mind and just hide in the corner. With the help of my family and friends, I was able to improve a little. When I saw this kindle e-book I knew I needed to read it. This book, hit me hard on the head and made me realize a lot of things I need to improve. I need to learn to love and appreciate myself first and just stop caring what other people think of me because in reality, they don't really care. What's important is how I see myself. Loved this book!"

— Lotte

OVERCOME
SOCIAL ANXIETY

Cure Shyness and
Talk to Anyone with Confidence

By Adam Rockman

WWW.EVOLVETOWIN.COM

Made in the USA
Las Vegas, NV
20 January 2022